To Sandra

Discover the Now

REFLECTIONS THAT ENCOURAGE

PAUL VITALE

Published by Vital Communications, Inc.
Post Office Box 2042
Little Rock, Arkansas 72203

Special acknowledgment is given to the authors of each individual prayer found within this manuscript, retrieved from the public domain. Your shared faith is an inspiration to us all.

Library of Congress Control Number 2013940885

ISBN 978-096661749-8

First Edition

With Special Thanks

With each endeavor comes the easy and complex. The process can be made smoother depending on those who surround you. A great deal of gratitude goes to Pam Bozeman for your valuable contribution to the overall design, typesetting, and content of this book. Your precision strengthened each element found on every page.

Printed in the United States of America

For my daughter

Sophia Grace

Your loving smile brings light to every space

For my wife

Jessica

Your loving support and encouragement are the difference

Preface

The hectic pace of the everyday has become the familiar versus the rare. One can easily become swept up by inundation and then, eventually, frustration. *Discover the Now—Reflections that Encourage* is the result of being familiar with the chaotic, but longing for the calm.

With the blessed birth of a new baby girl and at the recommendation of a colleague, the pastime of snapping photographs turned into occasions to decelerate into a more present state of mind. The joy of concentrating on the most opportune angles, lighting, and depth ultimately moved me to share with others what was transpiring right in front of my camera lens. The aesthetic experience demonstrated firsthand that all things occur in the now, if only I would slow down long enough to take notice. It is the smallest happenings that often carry the largest reminders, and thanks to that I am encouraged to encourage others not only through my individual collection of photography, but my personal quotations as well.

As you embark on the following pages, my wish is that you feel the rays of hope that this compilation is intended to shed. During a time when our world is in need of more encouragement than despair, more radiance than gloom, the photos taken and the quotes coined are offered to inspire. Enjoy the images, ponder the expressions, and take delight in conveying them to others when wanting to lift their spirits, too. It is my desire that you find as much pleasure in doing so as I have in the journey leading to the creation of this book.

It's up to you to discover the now.

~ Paul Vitale
Little Rock, Arkansas

*It is not where you
have been and what
you have traveled
through, it is where you
are going and how
many lives you'll touch
along the way.*

Don't ever underestimate the splendor of a kind word, a warm smile, or one simple act of generosity.

THOSE WHO ENTER LIFE'S ARENA EITHER "DO" WITH GREAT PASSION OR "BE" WITH UNWAVERING CONTENTMENT. THERE IS ALWAYS ROOM FOR BOTH.

When nothing is certain, anything is possible;
find your passions, discover your life.

WORDS UNSAID NEVER
SOLVE ANYTHING.

Lord, grant that I may always allow myself
to be guided by you,
always follow your plans,
and perfectly accomplish your holy will.
Grant that in all things,
great and small,
today and all the days of my life,
I may do whatever you may require of me.
Help me to respond
to the slightest prompting of your grace,
so that I may be
your trustworthy instrument for your honor.
May your will be done in time and eternity
by me, in me, and through me. Amen.

- St. Teresa of Avila

What will be the biggest achievement between your sunrise and sunset? Many have good intentions, but to finish is a choice.

When you begin treating people like people, they become people. No matter how large or small, your contribution of enthusiasm gives hope to others. The message being communicated leaves an everlasting mark!

It has often been debated how success is gauged. You pen the standards that measure your life's achievements.

The sea of simplicity
is often more treasured
by one in the midst
of turmoil. During
uncertain times, retool,
regroup, and re-energize.

ACHIEVEMENT IS THE RESULT OF POSITIVE HABITS BROUGHT TO LIFE.

A smile promotes good cheer and sound health to those who welcome it. Continue painting bright colors in the lives of others. Find your fun and be well!

TALENT IS CHEAP, BUT HARD WORK IS AT A PREMIUM.

A sturdy work ethic anchored
by commonsense values is hard
to overlook. When individuals
possess a sense of self-worth, it's
not difficult moving the pendulum
from marginal to memorable.

The seed of potential is planted in each of us; the direction it grows and for how long are up to you.

Incline us, O God,
to think humbly of ourselves,
to be severe only in the examination
of our own conduct,
to consider our fellow creatures
with kindness, and to judge of
all they say and do with that charity which
we would desire from them ourselves.
Amen.

- Jane Austen

The blossoms of
your legacy sprout
from the seeds
you plant
throughout a
lifetime.

A strong resolve results from a strong within.

No one who ever led a mighty charge or followed the persuasive cry of another reached the finish line without a piece or two of shattered resolve.

Any time there are two or more people engaged in dialogue, the possibility for discord exists. With this truth comes the reality that we can each be a peacemaker or troublemaker—the choice is ours.

SO MANY PASS
BY WITHOUT
A PAUSE, AND
THEN THERE
ARE THOSE
ONE OR TWO.

*With the passage of
one day to the next
comes this timely call:
Right your wrongs,
spread your joy,
leave your mark.
Whatever your
purpose, embrace it
completely!*

*In finding a way
to make others
feel as though they
matter, not only will
you motivate them,
they'll motivate you.*

THE WEIGHT OF WORDS,
EITHER NEGATIVE OR
POSITIVE, SHOULD NEVER
BE UNDERESTIMATED
REGARDLESS OF THE
SITUATION IN WHICH
THEY ARE SPOKEN.

Stretch the boundaries of your imagination; it's you who fuels the engine of your dream factory.

Larger successes are made up of smaller happenings.
What we do flows from who we are.

Lord, if your people

still have need of my services,

I will not avoid the toil.

Your will be done.

I have fought the good fight

long enough.

Yet if you bid me continue

to hold the battle line

in defense of your camp,

I will never beg to be excused

from failing strength.

I will do the work you entrust to me.

While you command,

I will fight beneath your banner. Amen.

- St. Martin of Tours

Go in search of all
the wonder waiting to
gush from your well
of curiosity.
To finish
you must
first begin.

Endure all moments of trial and sorrow with the belief that brighter days are on the horizon.

When others say that your aim is too high, don't become discouraged by their observations. No significant feat was ever achieved by aiming too low.

Our trials and
sorrows test us;
enthusiasm helps
breathe life back
into our sails !

TREPIDATION IMPEDES THE GROWTH OF A POISED AND CONFIDENT MIND.

When the rumble of a storm is approaching your threshold, stride from one day to the next with calm confidence and peaceful resolve, knowing that it's never so bad that it couldn't be worse.

THE GLOW
OF LIGHT IS
NOT ALWAYS
MEASURED IN
BRIGHTNESS,
BUT LONGEVITY.

The highs and lows of spectacular views are seen through the dusty haze of the everyday. The toughest opponent of a clear mind is the murkiness of fatigue.

No matter where you live or where you travel, this world revolves around those who occupy space and those who bring it to life.

Lord, when I am confused, guide me. When I am weary, energize me. When I am burned out, infuse me with the light of the Holy Spirit. May the work that I do and the way I do it bring faith, joy and a smile to all that I come in contact with today.

Lord, I thank you for everything you've done, everything you're doing, and everything you're going to do.

In the name of Jesus I pray, with much love and thanksgiving. Amen.

- Workplace Prayer

ENTHUSIASM
STRIKES A CHORD
THAT ECHOES
IN THOSE WHO
WANT TO
HEAR IT.
PRACTICE
WITH
PASSION,
PLAY WITH
PURPOSE.

As the
moonlight
meets the
dawn, never
expect
anything
less than the
unexpected.

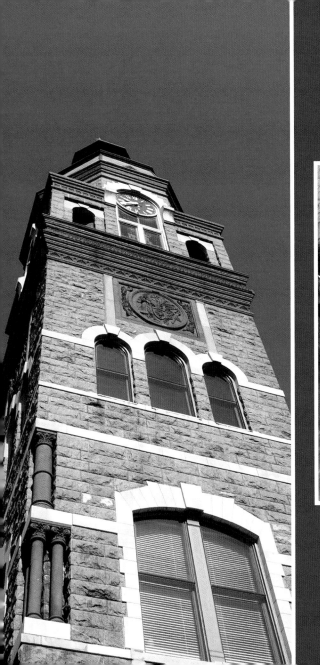

The mystery
of tomorrow,
coupled with
the arrival of
today, fuels the
excitement of
all that is
possible.

Come to expect as much from others as you do from yourself. If your expectations are met, be glad; if they are exceeded, rejoice.

LIFE IS GOOD WHEN YOU FIND THE GOOD IN LIFE!

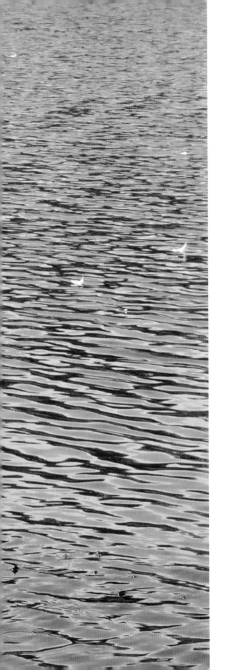

Get lost in the beauty
every now and then
so you never lose sight
of God's greatness.
Every day is a good
day to be inspired!

The road you travel will grow crooked and steep. Setbacks can be setups for enormous growth.

There is nothing more exhilarating than to encounter someone excited by what he or she does. Never discard the significance of energy flowing from one to another. A positive surge can produce favorable results.

As time quietly passes, be conscious of your contribution to this ever-changing world.

Lord, give us all the courage we need
to go the way you shepherd us,
that when you call we may go unfrightened.
If you bid us come to you across the waters,
that we may not be frightened as we go.
And if you bid us climb the hill,
may we not notice that it is a hill,
mindful only of the happiness of your company.
You made us for yourself, that we should travel with you
and see you at last in your unveiled beauty
in the abiding city, where you are light and happiness
and endless home. Amen.

- Bede Jarrett, O.P.

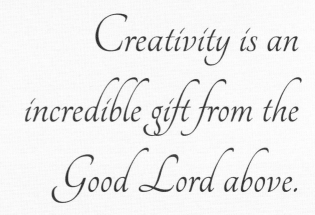

Creativity is an incredible gift from the Good Lord above. Welcome it, use it for the betterment of others, spread it fervently.

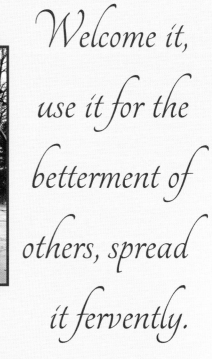

A man is a reflection
of his enthusiasm.

When a burst of
knowledge taps
at your mind's
door, capture
the moment
enthusiastically,
for it might not
knock so loudly
the next time.

THE WILL TO SUCCEED,
COUPLED WITH
DEDICATION TO
EXCELLENCE, ENABLES
A PERSON OF AVERAGE
ABILITY TO SURPASS
EXPECTATIONS.

DISCOVER A PATH THAT BRINGS JOY TO YOUR JOURNEY.

For every individual
who has pushed
limits and stretched
boundaries, I
commend you and
encourage you to
stay the course.

What was once known as common courtesy is not so common anymore. Exemplifying selflessness rather than selfishness can correct that. Never before has an abundance of politeness from one human being to another been so essential.

To dream means to live.
To live means to share.
To share means to
improve the place that
we call home.

*Erase the negative from your mind
and begin penciling in the positive.*

LEAVE YOUR MARK THROUGH
THE DREAMS YOU CHASE.

Lord Jesus,

I give you my hands to do your work,

my feet to go your way,

my eyes to see as you do,

my tongue to speak your words,

my mind that you may think in me,

my spirit that you may pray in me.

Above all, I give you my heart that you may

love in me all that you have created.

I give you my whole self that you may grow in

me, so that it is you, Lord Jesus, who live and

work and pray in me. Amen.

- Lancelot Andrewes

Inspired leaders are those who don't lead so much by words, but through their examples.

To the voice that casts doubt, respect its cautionary tone. To the voice that encourages mighty movement, appreciate its perspective. As the recipient of such wisdom, act accordingly... knowing that your life will only be lived once!

You attract
what you
project. Passion,
resilience, and
the willingness
to learn are
common
denominators
that equal
accomplishment.

Every individual
awakens to the
opportunity of a fresh
state of mind.

WE ALL POSSESS THE THUNDER OF FURY AND THE CALM BREEZE OF TRANQUILITY.

My profession has allowed me the privilege to travel the world and for that, I am most grateful. From large cities to small towns, I have caught a glimpse of spectacular sights and incredible storybook landscapes. However, as astonishing as the backdrops have been, one important truth has been revealed: No matter where you live or where you journey, this world revolves around those who occupy space and those who bring it to life.

It is my hope that the previous pages brought you enjoyment and served as a simple reminder of how discovering the now inspires fulfillment in every waking moment. Whatever it is, continue breathing life into each step along your journey, being encouraged to encourage others. I am finished chasing pictures and coining quotes for the moment, but my camera and pen will always be packed, ready to discover the now.

Also by Paul Vitale

Are You Puzzled by the Puzzle of Life?
Pass It On—Quotations for All Generations
Sell With Confidence—Unlock Your Potential

Titles may be purchased in bulk for educational, business, fund-raising, or promotional use. For information, call 501-663-1454.
www.paulvitale.com